# ADDRESS BOOK
# **SUNFLOWER**

The Pocket Size Address Book

www.journalsrus.com

Address Book Sunflower
© 2016 Ciparum LLC
All rights reserved.
ISBN-10:1-63589-070-5
ISBN-13:978-1-63589-070-9

# Table of Content

| Name | Page | | Name | Page |
|------|------|------|------|------|
| | | | | |
| | | | | |
| | | | | |
| | | | | |
| | | | | |
| | | | | |
| | | | | |
| | | | | |
| | | | | |
| | | | | |
| | | | | |
| | | | | |
| | | | | |
| | | | | |

| Name | Page | | Name | Page |
|------|------|--|------|------|
| | | | | |
| | | | | |
| | | | | |
| | | | | |
| | | | | |
| | | | | |
| | | | | |
| | | | | |
| | | | | |
| | | | | |
| | | | | |
| | | | | |
| | | | | |

THIS PAGE WAS
INTENTIONALLY
LEFT BLANK

**NAME**...................................................................................

ADDRESS..............................................................................

...............................................................................................

MOBILE # (Cell)................................................................

HOME #................................................................................

WORK #...............................................................................

FAX.......................................................................................

EMAIL..................................................................................

---

**NAME**...................................................................................

ADDRESS..............................................................................

...............................................................................................

MOBILE # (Cell)................................................................

HOME #................................................................................

WORK #...............................................................................

FAX.......................................................................................

EMAIL..................................................................................

---

**NAME**...................................................................................

ADDRESS..............................................................................

...............................................................................................

MOBILE # (Cell)................................................................

HOME #................................................................................

WORK #...............................................................................

FAX.......................................................................................

EMAIL..................................................................................

---

**NOTES:**

**NAME**........................................................................................

ADDRESS.................................................................................

.............................................................................................

MOBILE # (Cell)....................................................................

HOME #.................................................................................

WORK #.................................................................................

FAX...........................................................................................

EMAIL.....................................................................................

---

**NAME**........................................................................................

ADDRESS.................................................................................

.............................................................................................

MOBILE # (Cell)....................................................................

HOME #.................................................................................

WORK #.................................................................................

FAX...........................................................................................

EMAIL.....................................................................................

---

**NAME**........................................................................................

ADDRESS.................................................................................

.............................................................................................

MOBILE # (Cell)....................................................................

HOME #.................................................................................

WORK #.................................................................................

FAX...........................................................................................

EMAIL.....................................................................................

---

**NOTES:**

**NAME**..........................................................................................

ADDRESS..........................................................................................

.......................................................................................................

MOBILE # (Cell).............................................................................

HOME #.............................................................................................

WORK #............................................................................................

FAX.....................................................................................................

EMAIL................................................................................................

---

**NAME**..........................................................................................

ADDRESS..........................................................................................

.......................................................................................................

MOBILE # (Cell).............................................................................

HOME #.............................................................................................

WORK #............................................................................................

FAX.....................................................................................................

EMAIL................................................................................................

---

**NAME**..........................................................................................

ADDRESS..........................................................................................

.......................................................................................................

MOBILE # (Cell).............................................................................

HOME #.............................................................................................

WORK #............................................................................................

FAX.....................................................................................................

EMAIL................................................................................................

---

**NOTES:**

3

**NAME**..........................................................................

ADDRESS.....................................................................

.............................................................................

MOBILE # (Cell)..........................................................

HOME #....................................................................

WORK #....................................................................

FAX...........................................................................

EMAIL......................................................................

---

**NAME**..........................................................................

ADDRESS.....................................................................

.............................................................................

MOBILE # (Cell)..........................................................

HOME #....................................................................

WORK #....................................................................

FAX...........................................................................

EMAIL......................................................................

---

**NAME**..........................................................................

ADDRESS.....................................................................

.............................................................................

MOBILE # (Cell)..........................................................

HOME #....................................................................

WORK #....................................................................

FAX...........................................................................

EMAIL......................................................................

---

**NOTES:**

NAME..................................................................................

ADDRESS...............................................................................

...........................................................................................

MOBILE # (Cell)......................................................................

HOME #.................................................................................

WORK #.................................................................................

FAX........................................................................................

EMAIL...................................................................................

---

NAME..................................................................................

ADDRESS...............................................................................

...........................................................................................

MOBILE # (Cell)......................................................................

HOME #.................................................................................

WORK #.................................................................................

FAX........................................................................................

EMAIL...................................................................................

---

NAME..................................................................................

ADDRESS...............................................................................

...........................................................................................

MOBILE # (Cell)......................................................................

HOME #.................................................................................

WORK #.................................................................................

FAX........................................................................................

EMAIL...................................................................................

---

**NOTES:**

**NAME**...................................................................

ADDRESS............................................................

..........................................................................

MOBILE # (Cell)................................................

HOME #...............................................................

WORK #...............................................................

FAX......................................................................

EMAIL..................................................................

---

**NAME**...................................................................

ADDRESS............................................................

..........................................................................

MOBILE # (Cell)................................................

HOME #...............................................................

WORK #...............................................................

FAX......................................................................

EMAIL..................................................................

---

**NAME**...................................................................

ADDRESS............................................................

..........................................................................

MOBILE # (Cell)................................................

HOME #...............................................................

WORK #...............................................................

FAX......................................................................

EMAIL..................................................................

---

**NOTES:**

**NAME**..................................................................................
ADDRESS..............................................................................
.............................................................................................
MOBILE # (Cell)..................................................................
HOME #................................................................................
WORK #................................................................................
FAX......................................................................................
EMAIL..................................................................................

---

**NAME**..................................................................................
ADDRESS..............................................................................
.............................................................................................
MOBILE # (Cell)..................................................................
HOME #................................................................................
WORK #................................................................................
FAX......................................................................................
EMAIL..................................................................................

---

**NAME**..................................................................................
ADDRESS..............................................................................
.............................................................................................
MOBILE # (Cell)..................................................................
HOME #................................................................................
WORK #................................................................................
FAX......................................................................................
EMAIL..................................................................................

---

**NOTES:**

**NAME**............................................................................................

ADDRESS......................................................................................

...................................................................................................

MOBILE # (Cell)..........................................................................

HOME #......................................................................................

WORK #......................................................................................

FAX.............................................................................................

EMAIL.........................................................................................

---

**NAME**............................................................................................

ADDRESS......................................................................................

...................................................................................................

MOBILE # (Cell)..........................................................................

HOME #......................................................................................

WORK #......................................................................................

FAX.............................................................................................

EMAIL.........................................................................................

---

**NAME**............................................................................................

ADDRESS......................................................................................

...................................................................................................

MOBILE # (Cell)..........................................................................

HOME #......................................................................................

WORK #......................................................................................

FAX.............................................................................................

EMAIL.........................................................................................

---

**NOTES:**

**NAME**.................................................................................
ADDRESS.............................................................................
........................................................................................
MOBILE # (Cell)..................................................................
HOME #..............................................................................
WORK #..............................................................................
FAX.....................................................................................
EMAIL................................................................................

---

**NAME**.................................................................................
ADDRESS.............................................................................
........................................................................................
MOBILE # (Cell)..................................................................
HOME #..............................................................................
WORK #..............................................................................
FAX.....................................................................................
EMAIL................................................................................

---

**NAME**.................................................................................
ADDRESS.............................................................................
........................................................................................
MOBILE # (Cell)..................................................................
HOME #..............................................................................
WORK #..............................................................................
FAX.....................................................................................
EMAIL................................................................................

---

**NOTES:**

**NAME**............................................................................

ADDRESS...........................................................................

.......................................................................................

MOBILE # (Cell)..............................................................

HOME #.............................................................................

WORK #............................................................................

FAX....................................................................................

EMAIL...............................................................................

---

**NAME**............................................................................

ADDRESS...........................................................................

.......................................................................................

MOBILE # (Cell)..............................................................

HOME #.............................................................................

WORK #............................................................................

FAX....................................................................................

EMAIL...............................................................................

---

**NAME**............................................................................

ADDRESS...........................................................................

.......................................................................................

MOBILE # (Cell)..............................................................

HOME #.............................................................................

WORK #............................................................................

FAX....................................................................................

EMAIL...............................................................................

---

## NOTES:

**NAME**.................................................................................

ADDRESS............................................................................

..............................................................................................

MOBILE # (Cell)................................................................

HOME #..............................................................................

WORK #.............................................................................

FAX......................................................................................

EMAIL................................................................................

---

**NAME**.................................................................................

ADDRESS............................................................................

..............................................................................................

MOBILE # (Cell)................................................................

HOME #..............................................................................

WORK #.............................................................................

FAX......................................................................................

EMAIL................................................................................

---

**NAME**.................................................................................

ADDRESS............................................................................

..............................................................................................

MOBILE # (Cell)................................................................

HOME #..............................................................................

WORK #.............................................................................

FAX......................................................................................

EMAIL................................................................................

---

**NOTES:**

NAME.....................................................................................
ADDRESS............................................................................
.....................................................................................................
MOBILE # (Cell).................................................................
HOME #..............................................................................
WORK #.............................................................................
FAX......................................................................................
EMAIL...............................................................................

---

NAME.....................................................................................
ADDRESS............................................................................
.....................................................................................................
MOBILE # (Cell).................................................................
HOME #..............................................................................
WORK #.............................................................................
FAX......................................................................................
EMAIL...............................................................................

---

NAME.....................................................................................
ADDRESS............................................................................
.....................................................................................................
MOBILE # (Cell).................................................................
HOME #..............................................................................
WORK #.............................................................................
FAX......................................................................................
EMAIL...............................................................................

---

## NOTES:

**NAME**..................................................................................

ADDRESS.............................................................................

..............................................................................................

MOBILE # (Cell).................................................................

HOME #................................................................................

WORK #................................................................................

FAX.......................................................................................

EMAIL..................................................................................

---

**NAME**..................................................................................

ADDRESS.............................................................................

..............................................................................................

MOBILE # (Cell).................................................................

HOME #................................................................................

WORK #................................................................................

FAX.......................................................................................

EMAIL..................................................................................

---

**NAME**..................................................................................

ADDRESS.............................................................................

..............................................................................................

MOBILE # (Cell).................................................................

HOME #................................................................................

WORK #................................................................................

FAX.......................................................................................

EMAIL..................................................................................

---

**NOTES:**

**NAME**....................................................................................

ADDRESS...............................................................................

.............................................................................................

MOBILE # (Cell)....................................................................

HOME #..................................................................................

WORK #.................................................................................

FAX.........................................................................................

EMAIL....................................................................................

---

**NAME**....................................................................................

ADDRESS...............................................................................

.............................................................................................

MOBILE # (Cell)....................................................................

HOME #..................................................................................

WORK #.................................................................................

FAX.........................................................................................

EMAIL....................................................................................

---

**NAME**....................................................................................

ADDRESS...............................................................................

.............................................................................................

MOBILE # (Cell)....................................................................

HOME #..................................................................................

WORK #.................................................................................

FAX.........................................................................................

EMAIL....................................................................................

---

**NOTES:**

**NAME**..................................................................................
ADDRESS..............................................................................
.............................................................................................
MOBILE # (Cell)..................................................................
HOME #................................................................................
WORK #................................................................................
FAX.......................................................................................
EMAIL..................................................................................

---

**NAME**..................................................................................
ADDRESS..............................................................................
.............................................................................................
MOBILE # (Cell)..................................................................
HOME #................................................................................
WORK #................................................................................
FAX.......................................................................................
EMAIL..................................................................................

---

**NAME**..................................................................................
ADDRESS..............................................................................
.............................................................................................
MOBILE # (Cell)..................................................................
HOME #................................................................................
WORK #................................................................................
FAX.......................................................................................
EMAIL..................................................................................

---

**NOTES:**

**NAME**.......................................................................................

ADDRESS.......................................................................................

...................................................................................................

MOBILE # (Cell)............................................................................

HOME #........................................................................................

WORK #........................................................................................

FAX..............................................................................................

EMAIL..........................................................................................

---

**NAME**.......................................................................................

ADDRESS.......................................................................................

...................................................................................................

MOBILE # (Cell)............................................................................

HOME #........................................................................................

WORK #........................................................................................

FAX..............................................................................................

EMAIL..........................................................................................

---

**NAME**.......................................................................................

ADDRESS.......................................................................................

...................................................................................................

MOBILE # (Cell)............................................................................

HOME #........................................................................................

WORK #........................................................................................

FAX..............................................................................................

EMAIL..........................................................................................

---

**NOTES:**

**NAME**................................................................................

ADDRESS.........................................................................

....................................................................................

MOBILE # (Cell)...............................................................

HOME #...........................................................................

WORK #...........................................................................

FAX..................................................................................

EMAIL..............................................................................

---

**NAME**................................................................................

ADDRESS.........................................................................

....................................................................................

MOBILE # (Cell)...............................................................

HOME #...........................................................................

WORK #...........................................................................

FAX..................................................................................

EMAIL..............................................................................

---

**NAME**................................................................................

ADDRESS.........................................................................

....................................................................................

MOBILE # (Cell)...............................................................

HOME #...........................................................................

WORK #...........................................................................

FAX..................................................................................

EMAIL..............................................................................

---

**NOTES:**

**NAME**...........................................................................................
ADDRESS.....................................................................................
.....................................................................................................
MOBILE # (Cell)........................................................................
HOME #.......................................................................................
WORK #.......................................................................................
FAX.............................................................................................
EMAIL........................................................................................

---

**NAME**...........................................................................................
ADDRESS.....................................................................................
.....................................................................................................
MOBILE # (Cell)........................................................................
HOME #.......................................................................................
WORK #.......................................................................................
FAX.............................................................................................
EMAIL........................................................................................

---

**NAME**...........................................................................................
ADDRESS.....................................................................................
.....................................................................................................
MOBILE # (Cell)........................................................................
HOME #.......................................................................................
WORK #.......................................................................................
FAX.............................................................................................
EMAIL........................................................................................

---

**NOTES:**

**NAME**...................................................................................

ADDRESS.............................................................................

...........................................................................................

MOBILE # (Cell)...............................................................

HOME #..............................................................................

WORK #..............................................................................

FAX.....................................................................................

EMAIL.................................................................................

**NAME**...................................................................................

ADDRESS.............................................................................

...........................................................................................

MOBILE # (Cell)...............................................................

HOME #..............................................................................

WORK #..............................................................................

FAX.....................................................................................

EMAIL.................................................................................

**NAME**...................................................................................

ADDRESS.............................................................................

...........................................................................................

MOBILE # (Cell)...............................................................

HOME #..............................................................................

WORK #..............................................................................

FAX.....................................................................................

EMAIL.................................................................................

<u>**NOTES:**</u>

**NAME**..............................................................................................

ADDRESS.............................................................................................

.............................................................................................................

MOBILE # (Cell)................................................................................

HOME #...............................................................................................

WORK #................................................................................................

FAX.......................................................................................................

EMAIL..................................................................................................

---

**NAME**..............................................................................................

ADDRESS.............................................................................................

.............................................................................................................

MOBILE # (Cell)................................................................................

HOME #...............................................................................................

WORK #................................................................................................

FAX.......................................................................................................

EMAIL..................................................................................................

---

**NAME**..............................................................................................

ADDRESS.............................................................................................

.............................................................................................................

MOBILE # (Cell)................................................................................

HOME #...............................................................................................

WORK #................................................................................................

FAX.......................................................................................................

EMAIL..................................................................................................

---

**NOTES:**

**NAME**...................................................................................

ADDRESS.............................................................................

...........................................................................................

MOBILE # (Cell)...............................................................

HOME #.............................................................................

WORK #..............................................................................

FAX.....................................................................................

EMAIL................................................................................

---

**NAME**...................................................................................

ADDRESS.............................................................................

...........................................................................................

MOBILE # (Cell)...............................................................

HOME #.............................................................................

WORK #..............................................................................

FAX.....................................................................................

EMAIL................................................................................

---

**NAME**...................................................................................

ADDRESS.............................................................................

...........................................................................................

MOBILE # (Cell)...............................................................

HOME #.............................................................................

WORK #..............................................................................

FAX.....................................................................................

EMAIL................................................................................

---

**NOTES:**

**NAME**...................................................................................

ADDRESS............................................................................

...............................................................................................

MOBILE # (Cell)...........................................................

HOME #.......................................................................

WORK #.........................................................................

FAX...............................................................................

EMAIL...........................................................................

---

**NAME**...................................................................................

ADDRESS............................................................................

...............................................................................................

MOBILE # (Cell)...........................................................

HOME #.......................................................................

WORK #.........................................................................

FAX...............................................................................

EMAIL...........................................................................

---

**NAME**...................................................................................

ADDRESS............................................................................

...............................................................................................

MOBILE # (Cell)...........................................................

HOME #.......................................................................

WORK #.........................................................................

FAX...............................................................................

EMAIL...........................................................................

---

**NOTES:**

**NAME**................................................................
ADDRESS.............................................................
..........................................................................
MOBILE # (Cell)....................................................
HOME #................................................................
WORK #................................................................
FAX......................................................................
EMAIL.................................................................

**NAME**................................................................
ADDRESS.............................................................
..........................................................................
MOBILE # (Cell)....................................................
HOME #................................................................
WORK #................................................................
FAX......................................................................
EMAIL.................................................................

**NAME**................................................................
ADDRESS.............................................................
..........................................................................
MOBILE # (Cell)....................................................
HOME #................................................................
WORK #................................................................
FAX......................................................................
EMAIL.................................................................

**NOTES:**

**NAME**................................................................................

ADDRESS.............................................................................
..........................................................................................

MOBILE # (Cell)..................................................................

HOME #..............................................................................

WORK #..............................................................................

FAX......................................................................................

EMAIL.................................................................................

---

**NAME**................................................................................

ADDRESS.............................................................................
..........................................................................................

MOBILE # (Cell)..................................................................

HOME #..............................................................................

WORK #..............................................................................

FAX......................................................................................

EMAIL.................................................................................

---

**NAME**................................................................................

ADDRESS.............................................................................
..........................................................................................

MOBILE # (Cell)..................................................................

HOME #..............................................................................

WORK #..............................................................................

FAX......................................................................................

EMAIL.................................................................................

---

**NOTES:**

**NAME**.............................................................................
ADDRESS...................................................................................
.................................................................................................
MOBILE # (Cell)....................................................................
HOME #..................................................................................
WORK #...................................................................................
FAX..........................................................................................
EMAIL.....................................................................................

---

**NAME**.............................................................................
ADDRESS...................................................................................
.................................................................................................
MOBILE # (Cell)....................................................................
HOME #..................................................................................
WORK #...................................................................................
FAX..........................................................................................
EMAIL.....................................................................................

---

**NAME**.............................................................................
ADDRESS...................................................................................
.................................................................................................
MOBILE # (Cell)....................................................................
HOME #..................................................................................
WORK #...................................................................................
FAX..........................................................................................
EMAIL.....................................................................................

---

<u>**NOTES:**</u>

**NAME**..................................................................................

ADDRESS...........................................................................

................................................................................................

MOBILE # (Cell)..........................................................

HOME #.........................................................................

WORK #.........................................................................

FAX...................................................................................

EMAIL.............................................................................

---

**NAME**..................................................................................

ADDRESS...........................................................................

................................................................................................

MOBILE # (Cell)..........................................................

HOME #.........................................................................

WORK #.........................................................................

FAX...................................................................................

EMAIL.............................................................................

---

**NAME**..................................................................................

ADDRESS...........................................................................

................................................................................................

MOBILE # (Cell)..........................................................

HOME #.........................................................................

WORK #.........................................................................

FAX...................................................................................

EMAIL.............................................................................

---

**NOTES:**

**NAME**...................................................................................
ADDRESS.............................................................................
.............................................................................................
MOBILE # (Cell).................................................................
HOME #..............................................................................
WORK #...............................................................................
FAX.....................................................................................
EMAIL................................................................................

**NAME**...................................................................................
ADDRESS.............................................................................
.............................................................................................
MOBILE # (Cell).................................................................
HOME #..............................................................................
WORK #...............................................................................
FAX.....................................................................................
EMAIL................................................................................

**NAME**...................................................................................
ADDRESS.............................................................................
.............................................................................................
MOBILE # (Cell).................................................................
HOME #..............................................................................
WORK #...............................................................................
FAX.....................................................................................
EMAIL................................................................................

**NOTES:**

**NAME**................................................................
ADDRESS................................................................
................................................................
MOBILE # (Cell)................................................................
HOME #................................................................
WORK #................................................................
FAX................................................................
EMAIL................................................................

---

**NAME**................................................................
ADDRESS................................................................
................................................................
MOBILE # (Cell)................................................................
HOME #................................................................
WORK #................................................................
FAX................................................................
EMAIL................................................................

---

**NAME**................................................................
ADDRESS................................................................
................................................................
MOBILE # (Cell)................................................................
HOME #................................................................
WORK #................................................................
FAX................................................................
EMAIL................................................................

---

**NOTES:**

**NAME**..........................................................................................
ADDRESS...............................................................................
...................................................................................................
MOBILE # (Cell)..........................................................................
HOME #.......................................................................................
WORK #.......................................................................................
FAX.............................................................................................
EMAIL.........................................................................................

**NAME**..........................................................................................
ADDRESS...............................................................................
...................................................................................................
MOBILE # (Cell)..........................................................................
HOME #.......................................................................................
WORK #.......................................................................................
FAX.............................................................................................
EMAIL.........................................................................................

**NAME**..........................................................................................
ADDRESS...............................................................................
...................................................................................................
MOBILE # (Cell)..........................................................................
HOME #.......................................................................................
WORK #.......................................................................................
FAX.............................................................................................
EMAIL.........................................................................................

**NOTES:**

NAME.................................................................................

ADDRESS..........................................................................

.............................................................................................

MOBILE # (Cell)...........................................................

HOME #..........................................................................

WORK #..........................................................................

FAX.................................................................................

EMAIL............................................................................

---

NAME.................................................................................

ADDRESS..........................................................................

.............................................................................................

MOBILE # (Cell)...........................................................

HOME #..........................................................................

WORK #..........................................................................

FAX.................................................................................

EMAIL............................................................................

---

NAME.................................................................................

ADDRESS..........................................................................

.............................................................................................

MOBILE # (Cell)...........................................................

HOME #..........................................................................

WORK #..........................................................................

FAX.................................................................................

EMAIL............................................................................

---

## NOTES:

**NAME**................................................................................

ADDRESS.........................................................................

...................................................................................

MOBILE # (Cell).............................................................

HOME #...........................................................................

WORK #...........................................................................

FAX..................................................................................

EMAIL.............................................................................

---

**NAME**................................................................................

ADDRESS.........................................................................

...................................................................................

MOBILE # (Cell).............................................................

HOME #...........................................................................

WORK #...........................................................................

FAX..................................................................................

EMAIL.............................................................................

---

**NAME**................................................................................

ADDRESS.........................................................................

...................................................................................

MOBILE # (Cell).............................................................

HOME #...........................................................................

WORK #...........................................................................

FAX..................................................................................

EMAIL.............................................................................

---

**NOTES:**

**NAME**............................................................................

ADDRESS..........................................................................

..........................................................................................

MOBILE # (Cell)................................................................

HOME #.............................................................................

WORK #.............................................................................

FAX....................................................................................

EMAIL...............................................................................

---

**NAME**............................................................................

ADDRESS..........................................................................

..........................................................................................

MOBILE # (Cell)................................................................

HOME #.............................................................................

WORK #.............................................................................

FAX....................................................................................

EMAIL...............................................................................

---

**NAME**............................................................................

ADDRESS..........................................................................

..........................................................................................

MOBILE # (Cell)................................................................

HOME #.............................................................................

WORK #.............................................................................

FAX....................................................................................

EMAIL...............................................................................

---

**NOTES:**

**NAME**...................................................................................
ADDRESS...............................................................................
...........................................................................................
MOBILE # (Cell).......................................................................
HOME #...................................................................................
WORK #...................................................................................
FAX..........................................................................................
EMAIL.....................................................................................

**NAME**...................................................................................
ADDRESS...............................................................................
...........................................................................................
MOBILE # (Cell).......................................................................
HOME #...................................................................................
WORK #...................................................................................
FAX..........................................................................................
EMAIL.....................................................................................

**NAME**...................................................................................
ADDRESS...............................................................................
...........................................................................................
MOBILE # (Cell).......................................................................
HOME #...................................................................................
WORK #...................................................................................
FAX..........................................................................................
EMAIL.....................................................................................

**NOTES:**

**NAME**...................................................................................

ADDRESS........................................................................

........................................................................................

MOBILE # (Cell)........................................................

HOME #.......................................................................

WORK #.......................................................................

FAX...............................................................................

EMAIL..........................................................................

---

**NAME**...................................................................................

ADDRESS........................................................................

........................................................................................

MOBILE # (Cell)........................................................

HOME #.......................................................................

WORK #.......................................................................

FAX...............................................................................

EMAIL..........................................................................

---

**NAME**...................................................................................

ADDRESS........................................................................

........................................................................................

MOBILE # (Cell)........................................................

HOME #.......................................................................

WORK #.......................................................................

FAX...............................................................................

EMAIL..........................................................................

---

**NOTES:**

**NAME**..........................................................................

ADDRESS.......................................................................

........................................................................................

MOBILE # (Cell)..........................................................

HOME #........................................................................

WORK #........................................................................

FAX...............................................................................

EMAIL..........................................................................

---

**NAME**..........................................................................

ADDRESS.......................................................................

........................................................................................

MOBILE # (Cell)..........................................................

HOME #........................................................................

WORK #........................................................................

FAX...............................................................................

EMAIL..........................................................................

---

**NAME**..........................................................................

ADDRESS.......................................................................

........................................................................................

MOBILE # (Cell)..........................................................

HOME #........................................................................

WORK #........................................................................

FAX...............................................................................

EMAIL..........................................................................

---

**NOTES:**

**NAME**...................................................................................

ADDRESS...............................................................................

...............................................................................................

MOBILE # (Cell)...................................................................

HOME #.................................................................................

WORK #.................................................................................

FAX........................................................................................

EMAIL...................................................................................

---

**NAME**...................................................................................

ADDRESS...............................................................................

...............................................................................................

MOBILE # (Cell)...................................................................

HOME #.................................................................................

WORK #.................................................................................

FAX........................................................................................

EMAIL...................................................................................

---

**NAME**...................................................................................

ADDRESS...............................................................................

...............................................................................................

MOBILE # (Cell)...................................................................

HOME #.................................................................................

WORK #.................................................................................

FAX........................................................................................

EMAIL...................................................................................

---

**NOTES:**

**NAME**...........................................................................................
ADDRESS.......................................................................................
...................................................................................................
MOBILE # (Cell)............................................................................
HOME #.........................................................................................
WORK #..........................................................................................
FAX................................................................................................
EMAIL..........................................................................................

**NAME**...........................................................................................
ADDRESS.......................................................................................
...................................................................................................
MOBILE # (Cell)............................................................................
HOME #.........................................................................................
WORK #..........................................................................................
FAX................................................................................................
EMAIL..........................................................................................

**NAME**...........................................................................................
ADDRESS.......................................................................................
...................................................................................................
MOBILE # (Cell)............................................................................
HOME #.........................................................................................
WORK #..........................................................................................
FAX................................................................................................
EMAIL..........................................................................................

**NOTES:**

**NAME**...................................................................................

ADDRESS...............................................................................

.............................................................................................

MOBILE # (Cell)...............................................................

HOME #..............................................................................

WORK #...............................................................................

FAX........................................................................................

EMAIL..................................................................................

---

**NAME**...................................................................................

ADDRESS...............................................................................

.............................................................................................

MOBILE # (Cell)...............................................................

HOME #..............................................................................

WORK #...............................................................................

FAX........................................................................................

EMAIL..................................................................................

---

**NAME**...................................................................................

ADDRESS...............................................................................

.............................................................................................

MOBILE # (Cell)...............................................................

HOME #..............................................................................

WORK #...............................................................................

FAX........................................................................................

EMAIL..................................................................................

---

**NOTES:**

**NAME**...................................................................................

ADDRESS...............................................................................

...........................................................................................

MOBILE # (Cell).....................................................................

HOME #.................................................................................

WORK #.................................................................................

FAX.........................................................................................

EMAIL....................................................................................

---

**NAME**...................................................................................

ADDRESS...............................................................................

...........................................................................................

MOBILE # (Cell).....................................................................

HOME #.................................................................................

WORK #.................................................................................

FAX.........................................................................................

EMAIL....................................................................................

---

**NAME**...................................................................................

ADDRESS...............................................................................

...........................................................................................

MOBILE # (Cell).....................................................................

HOME #.................................................................................

WORK #.................................................................................

FAX.........................................................................................

EMAIL....................................................................................

---

**NOTES:**

**NAME**..................................................................................

ADDRESS...........................................................................

..............................................................................................

MOBILE # (Cell).............................................................

HOME #............................................................................

WORK #...........................................................................

FAX...................................................................................

EMAIL..............................................................................

---

**NAME**..................................................................................

ADDRESS...........................................................................

..............................................................................................

MOBILE # (Cell).............................................................

HOME #............................................................................

WORK #...........................................................................

FAX...................................................................................

EMAIL..............................................................................

---

**NAME**..................................................................................

ADDRESS...........................................................................

..............................................................................................

MOBILE # (Cell).............................................................

HOME #............................................................................

WORK #...........................................................................

FAX...................................................................................

EMAIL..............................................................................

---

**NOTES:**

**NAME**...................................................................................

ADDRESS..............................................................................

.........................................................................................

MOBILE # (Cell)..................................................................

HOME #...............................................................................

WORK #...............................................................................

FAX......................................................................................

EMAIL.................................................................................

---

**NAME**...................................................................................

ADDRESS..............................................................................

.........................................................................................

MOBILE # (Cell)..................................................................

HOME #...............................................................................

WORK #...............................................................................

FAX......................................................................................

EMAIL.................................................................................

---

**NAME**...................................................................................

ADDRESS..............................................................................

.........................................................................................

MOBILE # (Cell)..................................................................

HOME #...............................................................................

WORK #...............................................................................

FAX......................................................................................

EMAIL.................................................................................

---

**NOTES:**

**NAME**.................................................................................

ADDRESS.............................................................................

..........................................................................................

MOBILE # (Cell).................................................................

HOME #...............................................................................

WORK #...............................................................................

FAX......................................................................................

EMAIL.................................................................................

---

**NAME**.................................................................................

ADDRESS.............................................................................

..........................................................................................

MOBILE # (Cell).................................................................

HOME #...............................................................................

WORK #...............................................................................

FAX......................................................................................

EMAIL.................................................................................

---

**NAME**.................................................................................

ADDRESS.............................................................................

..........................................................................................

MOBILE # (Cell).................................................................

HOME #...............................................................................

WORK #...............................................................................

FAX......................................................................................

EMAIL.................................................................................

---

<u>**NOTES:**</u>

---

**NAME**.....................................................................
ADDRESS...............................................................
........................................................................
MOBILE # (Cell)....................................................
HOME #.................................................................
WORK #.................................................................
FAX.......................................................................
EMAIL..................................................................

---

**NAME**.....................................................................
ADDRESS...............................................................
........................................................................
MOBILE # (Cell)....................................................
HOME #.................................................................
WORK #.................................................................
FAX.......................................................................
EMAIL..................................................................

---

**NAME**.....................................................................
ADDRESS...............................................................
........................................................................
MOBILE # (Cell)....................................................
HOME #.................................................................
WORK #.................................................................
FAX.......................................................................
EMAIL..................................................................

---

**NOTES:**

**NAME**...........................................................................................

ADDRESS...................................................................................

...............................................................................................

MOBILE # (Cell)...................................................................

HOME #.................................................................................

WORK #.................................................................................

FAX..........................................................................................

EMAIL.....................................................................................

---

**NAME**...........................................................................................

ADDRESS...................................................................................

...............................................................................................

MOBILE # (Cell)...................................................................

HOME #.................................................................................

WORK #.................................................................................

FAX..........................................................................................

EMAIL.....................................................................................

---

**NAME**...........................................................................................

ADDRESS...................................................................................

...............................................................................................

MOBILE # (Cell)...................................................................

HOME #.................................................................................

WORK #.................................................................................

FAX..........................................................................................

EMAIL.....................................................................................

---

**NOTES:**

**NAME**..................................................................................

ADDRESS................................................................................

..............................................................................................

MOBILE # (Cell)......................................................................

HOME #..................................................................................

WORK #..................................................................................

FAX........................................................................................

EMAIL....................................................................................

---

**NAME**..................................................................................

ADDRESS................................................................................

..............................................................................................

MOBILE # (Cell)......................................................................

HOME #..................................................................................

WORK #..................................................................................

FAX........................................................................................

EMAIL....................................................................................

---

**NAME**..................................................................................

ADDRESS................................................................................

..............................................................................................

MOBILE # (Cell)......................................................................

HOME #..................................................................................

WORK #..................................................................................

FAX........................................................................................

EMAIL....................................................................................

---

**NOTES:**

**NAME**.........................................................................................

ADDRESS...........................................................................................

.........................................................................................................

MOBILE # (Cell).............................................................................

HOME #...........................................................................................

WORK #...........................................................................................

FAX..................................................................................................

EMAIL.............................................................................................

---

**NAME**.........................................................................................

ADDRESS...........................................................................................

.........................................................................................................

MOBILE # (Cell).............................................................................

HOME #...........................................................................................

WORK #...........................................................................................

FAX..................................................................................................

EMAIL.............................................................................................

---

**NAME**.........................................................................................

ADDRESS...........................................................................................

.........................................................................................................

MOBILE # (Cell).............................................................................

HOME #...........................................................................................

WORK #...........................................................................................

FAX..................................................................................................

EMAIL.............................................................................................

---

**NOTES:**

**NAME**...............................................................................

ADDRESS..........................................................................

...............................................................................................

MOBILE # (Cell)...........................................................

HOME #......................................................................

WORK #......................................................................

FAX.............................................................................

EMAIL.........................................................................

---

**NAME**...............................................................................

ADDRESS..........................................................................

...............................................................................................

MOBILE # (Cell)...........................................................

HOME #......................................................................

WORK #......................................................................

FAX.............................................................................

EMAIL.........................................................................

---

**NAME**...............................................................................

ADDRESS..........................................................................

...............................................................................................

MOBILE # (Cell)...........................................................

HOME #......................................................................

WORK #......................................................................

FAX.............................................................................

EMAIL.........................................................................

---

**NOTES:**

NAME...........................................................................................
ADDRESS.....................................................................................
...................................................................................................
MOBILE # (Cell).........................................................................
HOME #.......................................................................................
WORK #.......................................................................................
FAX..............................................................................................
EMAIL..........................................................................................

---

NAME...........................................................................................
ADDRESS.....................................................................................
...................................................................................................
MOBILE # (Cell).........................................................................
HOME #.......................................................................................
WORK #.......................................................................................
FAX..............................................................................................
EMAIL..........................................................................................

---

NAME...........................................................................................
ADDRESS.....................................................................................
...................................................................................................
MOBILE # (Cell).........................................................................
HOME #.......................................................................................
WORK #.......................................................................................
FAX..............................................................................................
EMAIL..........................................................................................

---

**NOTES:**

**NAME**..................................................................................

ADDRESS..........................................................................

..........................................................................................

MOBILE # (Cell).............................................................

HOME #............................................................................

WORK #............................................................................

FAX....................................................................................

EMAIL..............................................................................

---

**NAME**..................................................................................

ADDRESS..........................................................................

..........................................................................................

MOBILE # (Cell).............................................................

HOME #............................................................................

WORK #............................................................................

FAX....................................................................................

EMAIL..............................................................................

---

**NAME**..................................................................................

ADDRESS..........................................................................

..........................................................................................

MOBILE # (Cell).............................................................

HOME #............................................................................

WORK #............................................................................

FAX....................................................................................

EMAIL..............................................................................

---

**NOTES:**

**NAME**...............................................................................

ADDRESS.............................................................................

...........................................................................................

MOBILE # (Cell)....................................................................

HOME #................................................................................

WORK #................................................................................

FAX......................................................................................

EMAIL.................................................................................

---

**NAME**...............................................................................

ADDRESS.............................................................................

...........................................................................................

MOBILE # (Cell)....................................................................

HOME #................................................................................

WORK #................................................................................

FAX......................................................................................

EMAIL.................................................................................

---

**NAME**...............................................................................

ADDRESS.............................................................................

...........................................................................................

MOBILE # (Cell)....................................................................

HOME #................................................................................

WORK #................................................................................

FAX......................................................................................

EMAIL.................................................................................

---

**NOTES:**

**NAME**..................................................................................
ADDRESS............................................................................
..........................................................................................
MOBILE # (Cell)................................................................
HOME #..............................................................................
WORK #..............................................................................
FAX.....................................................................................
EMAIL................................................................................

**NAME**..................................................................................
ADDRESS............................................................................
..........................................................................................
MOBILE # (Cell)................................................................
HOME #..............................................................................
WORK #..............................................................................
FAX.....................................................................................
EMAIL................................................................................

**NAME**..................................................................................
ADDRESS............................................................................
..........................................................................................
MOBILE # (Cell)................................................................
HOME #..............................................................................
WORK #..............................................................................
FAX.....................................................................................
EMAIL................................................................................

**NOTES:**

NAME...........................................................................................
ADDRESS.....................................................................................
................................................................................................
MOBILE # (Cell).........................................................................
HOME #.......................................................................................
WORK #.......................................................................................
FAX............................................................................................
EMAIL.........................................................................................

NAME...........................................................................................
ADDRESS.....................................................................................
................................................................................................
MOBILE # (Cell).........................................................................
HOME #.......................................................................................
WORK #.......................................................................................
FAX............................................................................................
EMAIL.........................................................................................

NAME...........................................................................................
ADDRESS.....................................................................................
................................................................................................
MOBILE # (Cell).........................................................................
HOME #.......................................................................................
WORK #.......................................................................................
FAX............................................................................................
EMAIL.........................................................................................

**NOTES:**

**NAME**..............................................................................

ADDRESS...........................................................................

..........................................................................................

MOBILE # (Cell)................................................................

HOME #.............................................................................

WORK #.............................................................................

FAX....................................................................................

EMAIL...............................................................................

---

**NAME**..............................................................................

ADDRESS...........................................................................

..........................................................................................

MOBILE # (Cell)................................................................

HOME #.............................................................................

WORK #.............................................................................

FAX....................................................................................

EMAIL...............................................................................

---

**NAME**..............................................................................

ADDRESS...........................................................................

..........................................................................................

MOBILE # (Cell)................................................................

HOME #.............................................................................

WORK #.............................................................................

FAX....................................................................................

EMAIL...............................................................................

---

**NOTES:**

**NAME**..................................................................................

ADDRESS...........................................................................

...........................................................................................

MOBILE # (Cell)...........................................................

HOME #.........................................................................

WORK #..........................................................................

FAX.................................................................................

EMAIL............................................................................

---

**NAME**..................................................................................

ADDRESS...........................................................................

...........................................................................................

MOBILE # (Cell)...........................................................

HOME #.........................................................................

WORK #..........................................................................

FAX.................................................................................

EMAIL............................................................................

---

**NAME**..................................................................................

ADDRESS...........................................................................

...........................................................................................

MOBILE # (Cell)...........................................................

HOME #.........................................................................

WORK #..........................................................................

FAX.................................................................................

EMAIL............................................................................

---

**NOTES:**

**NAME**..............................................................................

ADDRESS............................................................................

.........................................................................................

MOBILE # (Cell)...............................................................

HOME #..............................................................................

WORK #..............................................................................

FAX......................................................................................

EMAIL................................................................................

---

**NAME**..............................................................................

ADDRESS............................................................................

.........................................................................................

MOBILE # (Cell)...............................................................

HOME #..............................................................................

WORK #..............................................................................

FAX......................................................................................

EMAIL................................................................................

---

**NAME**..............................................................................

ADDRESS............................................................................

.........................................................................................

MOBILE # (Cell)...............................................................

HOME #..............................................................................

WORK #..............................................................................

FAX......................................................................................

EMAIL................................................................................

---

**NOTES:**

www.ingramcontent.com/pod-product-compliance
Lightning Source LLC
Chambersburg PA
CBHW060511220326
41598CB00025B/3634